Who is Jim Butin?

Jim Butin is recognized as a tenth degree Black Belt by both the World Martial Arts Ranking Association and the American Karate Black Belt Association. He owns and operates National Karate and Tae Kwon Do, in Oklahoma City.

Jim started his Tae Kwon Do training in Fort Worth,Texas in November of 1965 at the age of 16 under Pat Burleson. Master Burleson's lineage comes from his association with Allen Steen from Dallas and Jhoon Rhee, who is considered to be the "Father of American Tae Kwon Do."

After making Black Belt in June of 1968, Jim competed in and won every major tournament that was prevalent in the Texas, Oklahoma, and Kansas area. He has won over 150 awards, all in fighting divisions. He won four National titles, and was rated as the #2 light heavy weight in the world by the PKA from 1974 to 1978. He was inducted into Official Karate's "Legion of Honor" and he is listed in four Martial Arts Halls of Fame including an inaugural induction to the Tae Kwon Do Hall of Fame, and can be found in the "Who's Who of Martial Arts".

Besides competing and winning the silver medal in the first World TKD Championships in Seoul, Korea in 1973, Jim also competed in Europe in 1974 with another famous U.S. team, which included Joe Lewis, Jeff Smith, Howard Jackson and Bill Wallace, against Germany, and the Netherlands. The team was undefeated in six separate contests. Jim is also a history general for the Sport Karate Museum.

When Jim walked away, he felt like he could benefit the sport by opening a Karate school. He worked hard and shared his knowledge and techniques with hundreds of talented students. Jim ran that very successful and profitable school for 47 years. He felt like he owed it to other schools, whether established or new, to share his experiences as both a competitor and a school owner.

DEDICATION

This book is dedicated to Grand Master J. Pat Burleson. Without his influence and guidance, none of this knowledge would have happened. He is my inspiration, my hero, my friend, and forever my instructor.

JIM BUTIN
KARATE
STORIES

From the "Blood and Guts" era of Tournament Karate

For additional information or to order copies of this book, visit

beyondthefighting.com

CONTENTS

One of my matches in Texas against Gary "Bull" Thomas

Foreword

In my experience, I have been blessed to be a part of martial arts history in the U.S. since 1966. As a 16-year old high school student starting classes with Master J. Pat Burleson in Ft. Worth, Texas, I was like a sponge from my very first class. I tried to absorb as much information as I could. There were not many books out in the world concerning karate, but I bought all that I could find. Mas Oyama's books including Advanced Karate, and Black Belt Magazine, were read until I wore the pages out. I read with fascination about the karate tournament stars, Chuck Norris, Joe Lewis, Mike Stone, Ron Marchini and others.

I started classes with my best friend and four other buddies in December of 1966 and I did not want any of them to get better than me, so I made sure I attended every class. I began my training at the General Dynamics Recreation Area in Ft. Worth, Texas. This was a recreation area for General Dynamics employees. I only had to pay $12.00 for a three month membership for once-a-week classes with employees. This was important because my parents would not pay for it and I could afford $12 from my $1 per week allowance that I saved. My parents were not employees of General Dynamics, but once I got past the security gate with one of my friends whose father was an employee, the guard began to recognize me. As I came by myself, he allowed me to enter. Fortunately the recreation area was a little lax in security otherwise I may not have been able to enjoy the experiences that I will share with you.

I was a tall skinny kid even at 16 years old, I was already 6'2" my current height, but weighed only 155 pounds soaking wet. The belt system at that time went from white belt to green belt and required three forms to test. I can't recall any other test requirements, but there may have been some. I remember that if you were great on your forms, you had the possibility to skip 8th KYU and go to 7th KYU green Belt. The testing concept was, that as a 10th KYU white belt, if you were that lousy at your forms, you may advance to 9th degree white belt as a partial advancement. The same plan was established for green belt at 8th and 7th and blue Belt at 6th and 5th. Exceptional students were considered for skipping a KYU level. I was never in that "exceptional" group. The events that I will reveal to you are in chronological order starting in 1966.

2

The "Baddest" Blue Belt you ever saw!

Early Training with J. Pat Burleson

One of the most influential classes that I attended under Grand Master J. Pat Burleson, was as a white belt. I knew that Pat Burleson's demeanor was macho and he-man, I had difficulty looking him in the eye. I did not know that he had won the first National Black Belt Championship in Washington D.C. in 1964, or that he was one of the fiercest and most respected Black Belts in the country. I just knew that when he spoke, you should listen, and then do what he said. In one class, I recall that he motioned for one of the men in line to step out for a demonstration of technique. That was not uncommon, but when Pat Burleson hit this guy with a reverse punch to the rib cage and the guy gasped and fell to the floor, my eyes were bugging out. The guy lay on the floor as Pat Burleson explained, "That's a reverse punch, if you do it right, that is what will happen every time (as he pointed to the guy on the ground)!" Then he told the guy to get back in line. I still to this day, don't know if that guy did something or say something to deserve Pat Burleson's retribution, or if he was just making a point. This guy was in the wrong place at the wrong time. I do not recall that guy ever attending a class again. The attitude of the day was "If you can't handle it, the door is right over there!" Today a martial arts studio that employs that old philosophy might be out of business in a short amount of time!

Early Tournament Experience

I competed in two tournaments as a blue belt in the "bare knuckle era" and I was as nervous as anyone could be in the competitions. It only took two points to win a match at that time by punch or by kick in two minutes. I won my first match and lost my second match in each of those events. I loved the winning, but hated the losses. I did not win a trophy in competition until I had made my Brown Belt and I remember that I wanted to win a trophy more than anything, I did not care if it was a 3rd or a 4th place, I just wanted one.

Brown Belt Tournament Success

I made Brown Belt and became an assistant instructor at GDRA and had the luxury of training under several of the top Black Belt in the Dallas/ Ft. Worth area. Pat Burleson, Chuck Loven, David Melville, Ron Moffet and Larry Covington were all Black Belt instructors that taught me at different

Pat Worley taking a drop front kick from me in the
GDRA karate room as brown belts

times at GDRA. When these guys could not be there, I was the instructor for the classes and on one occasion had as many as 75 people in class.
Finally I competed in a small tournament hosted by the GDRA in 1967. I won 1st place in the Brown Belt division against my best friend that I had started classes with. Only he and I were still in Karate classes, the other four of our buddies all quit the program. I could not believe the rush I received for this individual accomplishment. That trophy was the focal point of my day. Every day I cleaned it, admired it, and wanted more. This is where my competition karate story starts.

In testing for my 2nd Brown Belt level, nothing was notable about the test. Every one of Pat Burleson's belt exams were physically tough and involved a lot of sparring, which I loved. Many times I saw guys who were terrible at forms, or self defense demos like "one or three-step sparring," but when it came to sparring, if they could kick butt they would pass the exam. I know that Pat Burleson and most of the testing board would laugh or give a large smile when someone would get nailed with a good shot, but then he would stand up and yell to "Watch your contact!" So there were some mixed messages being sent to me. In my final match on the test, I was part of a "two against one match" against a man testing for his Brown Belt. During the match I slipped, or got knocked down, and fell on my back. As I rose up on my elbows in an attempt to get up, the guy I was sparring against turned and front kicked me in the same eye that had been ripped open before in a street encounter I was in, at that time I got cut open by a ring that a guy was wearing and did not get stitches, and of course it bled profusely. This time I did go to the emergency room at the hospital and get my four stitches that I should have had when the injury first occurred. I never had trouble with that eye again.

The highlight of my Brown Belt competition days were in Austin, Texas in 1968. I fought Pat Worley for 1st place in that event and I can't tell you about anything significant about the match except that I won. I had several people approach me and tell me that the match with Pat Worley was as good as the Black Belts fighting that day! I was blessed to be involved in training in this era with so many future top Black Belts in from the Ft. Worth/Dallas area. John and Pat Worley, Larry Carnahan, Bill Watson, Roy Kurban, Keith Yates, and many others that achieved notoriety came from this area.

I have included a great picture of one of my sparring sessions with Pat Worley in this book. Pat came over to the GDRA workout area and met me to spar one weekend afternoon. The picture captured me as I dropped to the floor when Pat threw a rear leg round kick at me. As I dropped to my back on the floor, I threw a front kick straight up to hit him in the groin. To do it was cool; to catch it on film was amazing.

The ability to read the attack that Pat had used against me and perform the technique that I scored with came to me from one of the aforementioned black belt instructors I had, Larry Covington. Larry was an early day genius when

6

it came to understanding body movement and conducting plans of counter attack. He could do anything to you in sparring that he put in his mind, he made his Black Belt from Pat Burleson in 16 months and was the only natural karate man I have ever known. He did things to me in sparring as a brown belt that I can't describe, he was awesome. Larry had some problem in using his skills on black belts in competition, as far as I know he never did well. Unfortunately, he never had a problem in using those skills on me!

Things rocked along for me and I continued winning in the Brown Belt division until one regional tournament in Ft. Worth that Pat Burleson had arranged in 1967. In that tournament I fought Roy Kurban and won the match, but I was not prepared for the next guy. It was George Smith, which means nothing to most people, but George was a biker, with a beard, about 240 lbs. and 6'2" or more, and he came from one of the Dallas karate studios under Allen Steen. Just to look at him would make you want to go the other way. Something about karate events made me want to try even against impossible odds, or maybe I just did not want to be embarrassed by withdrawing, or I was not smart enough to consider it. This was not just a special macho characteristic of mine, but it was the norm for all advanced belts in this era, you paid your money and took your chances. When the match started, I do not recall scoring a point on George, all I do remember is that he hit me in the throat with a rear leg round kick and knocked me off my feet. The match ended, I don't know if it was because I could not continue, or if I gamely survived (ran) until the two minutes expired! I could not talk clearly for a week or so after that event.
I really got popped.

About this time I had advanced to 2nd degree Brown Belt and kept training feverishly. I loved the workouts and couldn't wait to spar with anybody who could make me better. I heard that there was a belt exam that was scheduled to be in Dallas at one of Allen Steen's studios in a couple of months. I was pretty ignorant at age 17 about order, structure, and diplomacy. I never considered that it might not be right for me to go to that exam and test for 1st degree Brown Belt under Allen Steen even if he was not my instructor. After all, we were from the same system, used the same forms, and Pat Burleson and Allen Steen were the best of friends and trained together. I thought that we were all one big family. I did not even ask Pat

Burleson for permission to go to Dallas and take the exam. It was not meant to be a slam or an affront to Pat Burleson, I was simply clueless.

When I got there several of my friends were there too. Roy Kurban, Keith Yates and other Dallas karate guys that I knew were in attendance. Allen Steen called me over to visit with him and said to me," Does Pat Burleson know that you are here to test?" I answered, "Sure, I think so!" I knew that I had not discussed the possibility of testing with Mr. Burleson. Mr. Steen went into his office and called Mr. Burleson for a heads up notification on the situation. He returned to the main room and we proceeded with the test. Mr. Steen's testing was just as fight oriented as Mr. Burleson's and everything happened as I expected and anticipated. The testing was hard, but I passed to 1st degree Brown Belt that day. I never received a certificate from Mr. Steen, which I would have cherished. The reason I did not get a certificate is not clear, but most likely a circumstance like that had never occurred before or since. Since I was not from the Texas Karate Institute in Dallas, the certificate was not forwarded to me.

It's Time to step up!

Nothing was ever said to me by Mr. Burleson about the testing I had gone through in Dallas, but the next story made me wonder if I should have addressed that situation in advance of my next test. Mr. Burleson approached me at the end of a great workout one day and said "I think you should test for black belt on the next exam!" I had mixed emotions about the test to black belt. It seemed like I had just made my brown belt and I finally was enjoying success at competition sparring. Now I was winning trophies in the brown belt arena. I liked being a "Large Fish" in a small pond. To compete in black belt matches meant that I would be at the bottom of the food chain. I saw how the rookies, new to black belt fighting would be pounded on without mercy by the veterans. Remember this is long before the advent of safety gear, the only safety gear we wore at that time was a cup and supporter and an occasional mouthpiece.

I enjoyed playing the tournament circuit and I was always looking forward to the next event. I had placed or won in six tournaments in the brown belt division and I had developed a pretty good strategy to help me win. I always kept my eye out for George Smith, not for revenge, but because I did not want to dance with him again. As an observation, I noticed that if there was a tough competitor that you wanted to fight or if there was someone that you did not want to fight against again, you may never see that individual at future competitions. For whatever reason, people quit the martial arts or at least did not attend the competition sport events anymore.

What Does Not Kill You Makes You Stronger!

Now was the big day, I was going to examine for 1st degree black belt. I was never sure I could ever be a black belt until Mr. Burleson told me it was time to do it! The test day was June 2nd, 1968, 2 ½ years from the time I started my first karate class.

The test site was at Pat Burleson's American Karate Studio on Camp Bowie Blvd. in Ft. Worth, Texas. The studio wasn't large, but had great visibility on a busy city street. The building was pie shaped and the only 5,000 BTU air conditioner in the building was blowing on the examination table. The testing candidates gathered at the pointy end of the building to be called on when it was their turn to perform. It seemed like a ton of people were there for the testing. John and Pat Worley, Larry Carnahan, Bill Watson, and other tough brown belts were there to get a piece of me, or advance to their next level. The temperature in Ft. Worth in June was already over 100 degrees. I was young and at 18 felt like I could take on whatever was thrown at me. I had prepared for this test by working on some one step counter attacks. This portion of the test employed movements to be used against a partner that would attack you.

With control and light contact the testing party would dispatch his attacker and show his fighting skills. This area showing skills was normally required and I had observed these requirements from previous tests. I had spent hours devising super cool one step counters that no man had ever before seen! I was excited about the opportunity to show my counter attacks on this test after the forms were completed. I never enjoyed executing the patterns of blocking and striking in stances called "forms" and I never thought that I could perform them well. So I thought that the "one step sparring" would be an opportunity to get the judges to look favorably on me. That would help me get better scores to help pass the exam before the sparring section started. Right after I had completed my forms, Mr. Burleson said, *"it's time for sparring!"*

9

Part of me was disappointed that I was not able to show my special "one step sparring combinations" that I had spent so much time on. But another part of me was glad that I could show my sparring skills and save some energy.

One thing I had not considered from the exam I had witnessed with the three candidates on an earlier exam, was the fact that at least one of the candidates was always resting. If two candidates were fighting then one was resting, and each man did his forms, one at a time, which provided more rest for the other two. I failed to understand the brilliance of that concept, the only one testing for Black Belt at this time was me and there was no rest! Mr. Burleson always let the sparring go for as long as he wanted, it could be two minutes, longer, or shorter, just depending on the action or the energy he wanted you to spend. As most of us know that are from this era of karate training, a big part of your test was about "How bad do you want it?" If you get hit in the face, do you lay there and try to get sympathy, or do you get up on your feet, even if you can't see, and go some more?

I can't tell you how many matches I fought that day, I remember hitting Bill Watson with a solid body punch and knocking his air out, then Mr. Burleson stood up in anger yelling for me to, "Watch your contact." For a moment I was confused as I thought that was what I was supposed to do, and Bill Watson was nationally known as a top brown belt competitor. I sure did not expect him to give me any slack and go light on me with his punching and kicking skills. After many more matches, I really have no clue as to how many, my strength was gone. I was fighting two or three guys at once, I really can't remember. I just know that I had nothing left. I was on my knees, shaking my head, and I could not talk. I tried to say that I wanted to quit, because I did not think that I could go on. I really thought that death was possible if this test went much longer. It was the hardest thing that I had ever done. Then Mr. Burleson had someone stand me up, he then pointed to two guys and said, ***"Get him!"*** I doubt that I applied much effort to strike those guys, but fortunately for me, that was my last match.

I remember some people carried me outside and put me on the hood of a car. The car was pretty hot in the sun, but it felt cool to me to be out of that heat trap. I later wondered if my trip for testing in Dallas with Mr. Steen had a little "Payback" attached to it. I was told that Mrs. Burleson would not talk to Pat for a couple of days after that test because of the tough time he gave me. She thought it was too brutal. I don't know if she had ever seen a black belt test before. I was never as proud of any of my achievements as I was to receive my black belt on that day! Pat Burleson took the belt off of his waist and tied it around me. I still have that belt to this day hanging in my office.

I have heard of people being notified on a bulletin board, or receiving an e-mail that they have just been promoted to black belt. I will never understand how that award can mean anything! I just know that from my experience that day, the saying that I had heard, "What does not kill you will make you stronger," made perfect sense.

Whole New World!

My first Black Belt tournament was pretty easy. Only one other competitor, Bill Shaw from the Ft. Worth area at the GDRA gym showed up to compete along with me. I think that the advance promotion for the tournament was a little weak at getting the word out, but I was happy that the superstars were not there. I won 1st place and recognized that Bill Shaw was just as glad as I

was that no one else attended. Bill was like a lot of guys that I knew in that era, he was not very good, average at best, but he would suit up and do it because he was a Black Belt and he was there to do his best!

Enter Fred Wren!

My next event was in September 1968 at Pat Burleson's Texas State Championships in Ft. Worth. I lost my first match to Joe Alvarado from Austin, Texas. A significant event that affected my future was in the observation of Fred Wren from Allen Steen's schools in Dallas. Fred Wren was a legendary hitter. His goal was to destroy you and the points that he received for scoring were something that the judges gave him for beating the crap out of the other guy. On this day I saw Fred hit a strong player, named Carlton Morris from south Texas, so hard I couldn't believe it.

There was not supposed to be face contact in those days of bare knuckle fighting, but that doesn't mean it didn't happen. In fact, I learned early in my fighting training that if you were grabbed and about to be punched in the face, you should turn your face to point to the side so that the punch you were about to be hit with would hit the flat side of your face. That effort would keep you from being cut and save you from getting stitches in the emergency room at the hospital. If you were hit directly to the face on the eyebrows, cheekbone or chin line you probably would get gashed and would need stitches or other medical attention. I learned that information the hard way, because I have had stitches on each eye, under my chin and on my hand from knocking a guy's tooth out.

Anyway, as Carlton moved in to score on Fred, he ran into a ridge hand on the side of his neck that made Carlton turn upside down and land head-first on the concrete slab floor during the tournament. Carlton was out cold, and at the time it seemed like an easy call for excessive contact against Fred. Disqualifications were rare in Black Belt fighting, but this looked like a good call for one against Fred. When Carlton was revived, they got some ice for the goose-egg swelling on his head. It was determined that Carlton could not continue, and since he was moving toward Fred in his attack, he was guilty of moving into the shot and contributed to his own contact. Therefore, Fred would not be disqualified and would continue in the bracket. Fred was not guilty of excessive contact. Wow! When I saw that whole scene transpire I realized that I was in the cage with the big dogs. I was just glad that I was not in there with Fred that day.

At my next tournament in Dallas my nightmare came true! Since I was tall and skinny, I always strived to compete in the light-weight division. This would allow me a reach advantage with my long arms and legs. That was true until they called my name and then called Fred Wren. Chuck Norris was the center official and it still only took two points to win a match. The judges would not call a point that did not clearly land with enough impact that it could hurt someone. Two out of three judges had to confirm the point or it was not awarded. So it was not uncommon for a match to go into overtime in order to determine the winner. That was not the case this time. When the match started Fred was on the attack. His favorite and most effective attack was to grab your sleeve, slam a round kick into you about stomach high and then follow up with a reverse punch to the head or body. Fred would then repeat the whole process over and over until you collapsed. All the while he was pulling or pushing you to keep you off balance as he continued to slam punches into you. Somehow, mostly by luck, I threw a round kick at his body as he reached to grab me and I hit him.

I was laying on the floor at Fred's feet while he punched me over and over, the judges had to pull him off of me. Chuck Norris asked for points and the majority of the judges called my round kick, because I struck first. I was partly happy, but very scared about what may happen next.

As Chuck Norris restarted the match, Fred again grabbed my gi and started his normally successful combo of raining down damage, like he had done to so many guys before. Again I scored with my desperation round kick as he reached for me. Again, the judges had to pull him off my prone body and I returned to my feet. I saw that the flags were held up, which were used to determine the competitor who had scored. Either a red or white flag showed me to be the majority winner. Chuck Norris was a little hesitant to award me the point and questioned the scorekeeper as to how many points had been scored. Fred responded, *"That's his second point and the match is over!"*

*Skipper Mullins and I in the US Championships
in 1969 with Mike Stone as the referee*

I reached to shake Fred's hand, but he turned away in disgust and left the ring. I went on to fight Skipper Mullins in the finals that night and finished third in the tournament after losing in overtime.

Skipper was always friendly to me and since we were built similarly, I studied many of his bouts to try and use some of his strategies. I determined at that time, Skipper's kicking skills and experience in the ring were far superior to mine, but I knew I could get better. I only fought Skipper two times and each time I lost to him in overtime bouts.

Fred Wren is Going to Kill You!

I was excited about my experience and victory from that event and was moving forward, when I was contacted by one of my Black Belt friends, Harold Gross. Harold trained in the same karate school as Fred and was a regular sparring partner for Fred. He asked me if I was planning to fight in the next big tournament in Dallas, the U.S. Karate Championships hosted by Allen Steen. I replied that definitely I was planning to go and compete.

Harold said, *"Don't go, Fred is drawing pictures of you on the heavy bag and beating it up in every class!"* He makes guys fight him throwing round kicks like you do and then he proceeds to destroy everyone in class!" I asked Harold to talk to Fred and let him know that the last fight was an accident. Harold said, *"You can't tell Fred anything, his mind is made up! Just don't go!"* Well, I understood what Harold was saying to me, but I went anyway. The U.S. Championships in Dallas was one of the biggest events in the country. When the lightweight Black Belts lined up there must have been thirty or more guys ready to fight in my weight class. I watched Fred go to the front of the line where they started taking names to make up the competition bracket. I went to the end of the line to stay as far away from Fred as possible. As the eliminations progressed and the line got shorter, Fred kept winning of course, and I also stayed in the hunt and won my matches.

Finally, there were four of us left for the finals that night. Fred Wren was bracketed to be against Douglas Hughes from Lubbock, Texas, and Harold Gross was charted to be against me. As we drew closer to the time to compete, Harold came to me and said, *"You better let me win! Fred is going to kill you!"* I knew that his statement was entirely possible since this

14

was the finals and no one ever got disqualified in the finals for excessive contact on the big stage. Fred beat Douglas Hughes, and I could not just let Harold beat me, so that means I won.

Now the stage was set for a first place bout in the Black Belt lightweight fighting division in the United States Karate Championships. I had never been in a situation before like the one I was faced with. I would like to say that I approached the ring with confidence and knew that I could win against a tough opponent no matter how tough and brutal he could be. After all, I won once before against this guy! Nope, it was nothing like that. I was sure that I was about to die.

When we bowed in to each other, all I could think about was to keep my hands up and survive. I probably threw two offensive techniques at Fred for the whole match. I did not try to win. He beat me easily; I was actually mentally beaten before we bowed in. After the match, I realized an emptiness and disappointment from my lack of participation and commitment from that match that I cannot express. Fred Wren did not kill me, I was still alive, my teeth were intact, and I was not bleeding. I then had to ask myself, what was I going to do the next time I had to get in and compete against Fred? I decided that I would not put my tail between my legs again. If I were to fight Fred Wren in the future, then it would really have to be a fight, because I hated the way the result of that encounter made me feel about myself. I knew that I had ability, and I loved the tournaments, and I was not going to quit, so this fear that I had must be dealt with.

The next time that Fred Wren and I fought each other was in Houston, Texas that next summer in 1969. This time I had done my homework. Not one practice session or sparring workout went by without my thoughts concentrated on what I must do to be competitive with Fred Wren in the next encounter. When I saw Fred at the tournament, I was not looking forward to the battle that we would have that day, but I was mentally and physically prepared to fight him. I don't remember anyone else I fought that day, Fred was my focal point. We fought for 1st place in the Summer Karate Olympics, hosted by George Minshew. I remember that I was concerned, and awed, about how fast Fred would come across the line, get into your space, then grab you and start beating the tar out of you in his fighting attack. I had developed a pretty good turning back kick counter attack during this era

15

and had put a lot of guys on the floor from impact to the body after they had pressed an offensive attack against me. I did not think that I could hit Fred with that technique, so I decided to step away in the opposite direction as the attack began. To my attacker, that made it look like I was running. I knew Fred had seen that look from me before, and I was hoping that if Fred paused in his attack, I could create enough distance to allow me to hit him with the turning back kick. It worked! I hit Fred flush in the gut with the strike. The fact that he was moving into the strike amplified the power that he was struck with and I knocked his air out. Fred was more cautious for the rest of the match and I was glad. Fred still won the match and I took 2nd place in the tournament, but I knew I had earned his respect and more importantly, I had earned my own respect back! I was so pleased about this fight that I vowed that no one would ever psyche me out in the future.

Later in 1970, Fred Wren and I fought for the final time in New Orleans, Louisiana at Takiyuki Mikami's All South Karate Championships. Fred and I fought for 1st place again, this time I was in control of the match and won the tournament and defeated the toughest karate competitor I had ever faced. I cannot express how excited I was about this victory. I also feel sad for the current generation of young Black Belts that are getting started in competition fighting in this current era. I do not believe that the opportunity exists for current Black Belt competitors to experience the lessons that I learned. I was able to see my growth into a man and I was fortunate enough to experience and battle through these problems as a 19-year old Black Belt.

The contact in today's events is watered down from the days I experienced. Disqualifications are now occurring for contact that would have been required to get a point in those "bare knuckle" days. Many of today's events have rules that allow points to be scored for just getting close. I believe that the current new Black Belts are missing out because they will never have the opportunity or challenge to face a "Fred Wren" in their future.

Chuck Loven

As I mentioned earlier, I had observed Chuck Loven as he tested for Black Belt and while he instructed some classes in which I attended in the late 60's. Chuck was as hard as a rock. He was the kind of guy that I thought that you could not hurt with a baseball bat. I fought Chuck in a small regional tournament as a Black Belt in Fort Worth in 1969 and I won 1st place with Chuck getting 2nd place and Bill Watson getting 3rd place. I also fought him in the U.S. Championships in Dallas in 1970 and took 3rd place, while he advanced and won 2nd place in that event. The pictures shown here were from that fight. The last time that we fought, was in Houston at the Karate Olympics held by George Minshew. This time it was for 1st place and the Grand Championship match was scheduled for three two minute rounds. I always respected Chuck Loven's power and ability, but I knew that his training consisted more on cigarettes and cold beer than mine did. By the third round, Chuck was behind on points, and breathing hard. I won the Grand Championship by staying out of his way and letting time expire.

Don't Be Predictable!

I mentioned my long time friend, Harold Gross in the previous story. Harold and I hung out on occasion and competed at various events in Colorado, Texas, and even California. One day Harold called me at my Karate Studio in Denton, Texas and wanted to come in to spar with me. I said "Sure, come on by and we will fight for a while." When Harold arrived we spent about an

Chuck Loven and I in the finals of the
1970 US Championships in Dallas

hour or so sparring, and I pretty much had my way with Harold. I hit him with all of my best combinations and techniques that I had been working on. I had a great time! We said our good-byes and Harold acted embarrassed about the sparring session, he was always a pretty humble guy.

A few weeks later, Harold called me again and wanted to know if he could come back and spar with me again. Remembering the last sparring encounter I said "Sure, come on in!" I expected the same result that had occurred earlier and proceeded to use the same techniques and strategy that I had employed with Harold previously. Surprise! Harold had gone back to Dallas and dissected all of my attacks, combos, defensive strategies and taken them completely apart.

Harold Gross

About every six months, I endeavored to change up my attack combinations and sparring strategies because of Harold Gross!

This sparring session was nothing like the one before, Harold stopped all of my attacks, and was the guy doing all of the hitting. I was astounded that he could figure out my stuff and shut me down as quickly as he did that day! I clearly understood that if Harold could do that to me, other top competitors could also find ways to control my strategies and anticipate my techniques and combinations. Because of that experience, Harold taught me not to be predictable, and I worked to change my methods and rotate my list of tournament techniques and strategies so that I was not so obvious in my skill set.

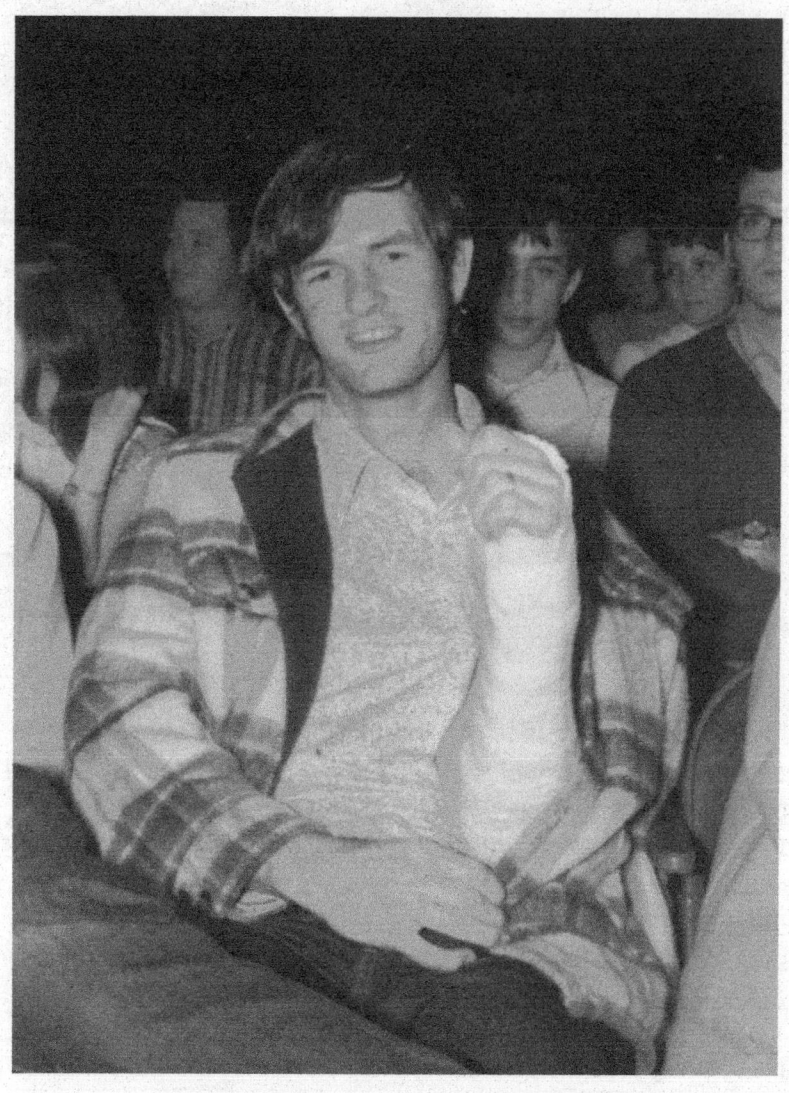

Bad day at the 1972 US Championships

I Broke My Arm?

In 1972, the first big event of the year was the U.S. Championships in Dallas. I had trained hard and was getting more well-known in karate events in the region. I had lost to Bill Wallace for the heavyweight title in 1971 and I was gunning to be the 1st place winner this year. I remember winning my first two or three matches cleanly. It only took three points to win and I beat my first two or three opponents three to nothing.

Then I drew another tough guy from south Texas, Daryl Stewart. I had fought Daryl before and won. I knew the match would be tough, but I was confident that I could win again. This match was the last match to qualify for the finals that night. I started strong and was ahead two points to zero and keeping my string of no points scored against me intact. Then Daryl threw a rear leg round kick at me which I blocked by raising my left arm vertically in front of my body. When he hit it hard, I immediately felt weak and my arm hurt in the clash. Mike Stone was the center official, Daryl received a point for another strike, and then Mike Stone restarted us immediately. I remember thinking that something was different. Now I was just standing around and not moving very effectively. Then Daryl threw another rear leg round kick that impacted my blocking arm in the same manner as before. This time I knew something was wrong. As I touched the contact area on my left arm with my other hand and rotated my wrist, I could feel the bones did not connect. The ulna, the small bone in my forearm was broken. Mike Stone ushered us to keep fighting. I looked at him and said, "I think I broke my arm!" He then had us bow out, Daryl took the victory and went to the finals, and I went to the emergency room.

I was 22 years old when these events took place. I noticed that I was getting injured too often. Previously, I had stitches over each eye, Tim Voight from Ed Daniels' school had knocked my tooth through my lip and I took some stitches, Roger Carpenter gashed my chin that took some stitches, and I had exploratory surgery on my left hand and ten stitches in my knuckle after cutting my hand from hitting Jim Miller from New Orleans in the mouth. Now, I have a busted arm. Emergency room costs back in the 70's are nothing like they are today, but I just couldn't afford to go to a hospital anymore. I told myself that I would compete in three more events and if anything bad happened to me in those tournaments, I would quit karate competition.

Fortunately I competed in three more events and won a 2nd and two 1st place awards and did not visit an emergency room again. I decided that I just had a bad run of luck!

National Black Belt Success

I also developed analytical traits to use against other competitors for myself. By analyzing guys that I thought I might have the opportunity to fight in the future, I thought that I would be a step ahead and have the advantage. When Professional Karate Magazine came out in 1973, it listed the top 20 Black Belt competitors in the United States. I was fortunate enough to make the #17 spot in the first issue. I looked at the guys ranked ahead of me and immediately made a list of the guys that I knew I could beat, the guys that I thought I could beat, and the guys that I hoped I could beat. After my experiences with Fred Wren, I believed that I could beat anyone in the rankings - no matter what their skill level was. The next issue, I advanced in the rankings to #11, and I advanced to #9 in the following issue. I always felt that any of the men in the top five could be #1 and I wanted to be one of them.

I remember that at first my goal in karate tournaments was to just have a trophy. After I won some third and fourths, I decided that the only winners were the ones who earned a 1st or a 2nd place award, and I didn't want to settle for anything less. After I had my share of the 1st and 2nd place trophies, I decided that there was only one winner - the guy who got 1st place. I wanted that to be me. Then with my success in Texas, I wanted to test the waters in Kansas, Oklahoma, Colorado and other karate events regionally. When I won there, I expanded and looked toward national competition. So naturally, when the Professional Karate Magazine rankings first appeared in 1973, I wanted to go where the big boys were and see if I could handle it and win nationally. I had fought against some of the top men in the nation during this time, Skipper Mullins, who I fought against twice and lost in overtime to him both times. Roger Carpenter the "Kansas Warhorse" I fought two times and won once. Fred Wren, from my previous stories, I had two out of four victories. Jeff Smith, I had fought five times and won three times, but he beat me for the PKA light heavyweight title in May of 1975 by a TKO in the fifth round. I had the honor to compete against Joe Lewis in Houston in the Karate Olympics in 1974 for 1st place and lost by a score of 4 to 2.

It always bothered me that I did not handle my one opportunity better with Joe Lewis. After all he was an icon, and one of the first men I had read about in the Karate magazines when I was a beginner. I made a rookie mistake that affected the outcome of my match with Joe. During this era, I had a front leg round kick to the groin which could not miss. With five judges in our match, Joe and I faced each other right foot forward, with the chief referee to my left. I quickly hit Joe with the round kick to the groin. He then countered me by hitting my jaw with a front hand ridge hand. The flags raised had two judges calling for my round kick to score, and three judges calling for his ridge hand to score. Even though I believed that my kick scored first, the judge's position gave him the advantage. Understanding ring strategy and judge's position, meant that at this point, I should have circled around Joe and shifted my position with my right leg forward stance to be on the side of the vision of the three judges instead of the side of the two judges that I had previously been in. But no! I stayed in the same position, I again hit Joe in the groin first and received another ridge hand to the jaw from him and another majority of flags were raised for Joe again. I finished the match 4 to 2 and lost, but I know I could have done much better.

Joe Lewis

In 1970 Allen Steen hosted the famous kickboxing card with Joe Lewis, Ed Daniel, Jim Harrison, Victor Moore and others. He also held a tournament during the day with the finals to be held that evening for awards and prizes called the "Hai Karate Open" Karate Championships. I was there to compete in the Black Belt fighting. Just after the brackets were filled in with the fight pairings, I saw the guy that I was scheduled to fight in my first match, Ray Klingenberg. Ray approached Joe Lewis to talk. Joe didn't know who I was and neither did my opponent. I stood around within earshot and heard Joe ask who Ray's first match would be. He said that it was some local guy named Butin. Joe told him that as soon as we bowed in, Ray should rush me and punch me right in the face. The judges would give me a point for face contact, but they would not disqualify him here in Texas. Joe said that would shake me up and that he would win the match easily after that. I moved away from their conversation and weighed the content of the discussion that they had. I believed that it was a great plan. When the scorekeeper called our names up to compete we bowed in to start the match. I quickly rushed over and punched Ray right in the mouth. He got a point for face contact, he obviously was shaken up from the contact and I easily won the match after that! The story for my match in the finals follows next.

Roy Kurban

Roy Kurban and I had quite a history in the early days of competition. Roy was about the same height and weight as I was. We had ample opportunity to compete against each other and we attended the same events. I won against Roy two times as a brown belt. And I bested Roy two out of three times in the black belt division. One event was for 1st place in the "Hai Karate Open" Karate Championships in Dallas, Texas when Joe Lewis fought Ed Daniels in the kickboxing show following the point tournament.

My first match in the finals against Steve Fisher
from California in the 1972 Colorado Open

I was getting married in Denver, Colorado the very next week end and wanted to win this tournament because the 1st place winner won a paid in full trip to Acapulco, Mexico. I figured that this would be the greatest honeymoon a guy could get. Roy was scheduled to leave for Korea for his tour of duty in the armed service and he decided that he needed this trip for rest and relaxation before he was shipped out. We both had our reasons to win, I don't remember what the total score of our match was, but I do remember wondering what Roy was doing as I enjoyed the cuisine and lay on the beach in Acapulco.

The next time we fought each other was in Denver, Colorado at Jim Harkins "Colorado Open" Karate Championships. I had won the tournament the previous year and was defending my title in July of 1972. Earlier that February, I had broken my arm against Daryl Stewart in Dallas at the US Championships and this was the first event that I competed in after my cast was removed. I remember that my arm was still tender and that I wore a rubber sleeve over my forearm to protect the area. My first match in the finals was against Steve Fisher, a Mike Stone Black Belt from California. I won against him. The final match was against Roy Kurban. Roy sized me up and we fought for a while. When Roy threw a hard round kick to my sore arm, it may not have been intentional, but I took it as an attempt to win at all cost. From Roy's perspective, he was there to win and he probably was just attempting to score. I would probably have done the same thing if the roles were reversed. I lost the match and took it personally.

I trained hard for the next couple of months thinking about how I would fight Roy Kurban the next time we met. Then Pat Burleson's "Texas State Championships and Tournament of Champions" in Ft. Worth came around in October of 1972. My first match was with Roy Kurban. I was very focused on Roy and I wanted to win badly. I had worked out hard to get my arm ready for the event. I remember that I scored three fast punches to his face and won the match three to nothing in a very short time. That was the last time that Roy and I got to fight each other.

This was also about the time that Roy was involved in a bitter dispute against Allen Steen over the opening of Roy's new karate school. Roy had been an instructor in Arlington, Texas in a Texas Karate Institute location

Jump Side Kick "Back In the Day!"

owned by Allen Steen in Arlington. The problem was that Roy opened his location only a mile or two from Mr. Steen's studio and all of the students naturally wanted to go to class where their instructor was teaching. Roy has a very likeable personality, so obviously the students wanted to be where he was and they flowed to his location.

Demetrius Havanas was hosting a tournament and Roy and I both had intentions of competing in his event. Pat Burleson approached me and asked me at the tournament to take a stand concerning Roy's action to go against his instructor by opening up a studio to compete directly against him in the same area. I chose to support Allen Steen and his position because I felt it was the right choice. I announced to the black belts that were lining up to compete, that if Roy Kurban was allowed to compete that day, then I would withdraw from the competition. Several other black belts decided to make the same choice and sided with my position. Roy felt bad about the division amongst the black belt competitors and the politics, but eventually he withdrew from the event and Roy did not compete in any of the area tournaments for quite a long time.

Dennis Gotcher

Competition was still the joy of my karate world and I remember attending many events and meeting a lot of people. One guy was Dennis Gotcher, who had a karate studio in Waco, Texas at the time. Dennis had been one of my white belt students in the classes I taught at Tarrant County Jr. College in the late 60's while I was a student there. He and I parted from the school environment and he continued his training somewhere else. After he made his black belt, I fought Dennis in a tournament somewhere in Texas, and beat him. One of my bread and butter techniques in competition at the time was a hook sweep to the knee that I had perfected from Takayuki Mikami's seminar that Master Burleson had set up previously in Ft. Worth, Texas. I'm sure I used it on Dennis Gotcher for that win. We were in the next karate event, probably in Dallas at the US Championships, and he approached me and told me that I had better not try to sweep his leg if we fought that day because he had a counter attack that would wipe me out.

After my experience with Harold Gross, I was not so sure that he did not have a good counter to use against me. I was cautious in our match until I was ahead by a couple of points, and then I had to know. I swept his leg, banged him in the back of the head with a punch and won the match. I don't doubt that Dennis had his sparring partners sweep his leg in practice and that he had developed a good counter attack, but the difference was they didn't have it perfected as I did with speed and timing. The effectiveness of the front leg sweep that I had learned from Mr. Mikami was not just to kick a man's leg to break his balance, but to pull myself behind him to gain a position advantage and to punch him in the head or body after I had turned his hips and widened his stance. Most competitors I faced did not have an answer for this type of technique.

First World Tae Kwon Do Championships

Sometime in late 1972, the word came around about a tournament in Dallas that would qualify a guy to go to Korea and compete on a US team in Seoul all expenses paid.

I showed up to compete in Richardson, Texas, and there was a ton of other black belts there who also wanted a spot. I remember wining one or two

26

matches, when I drew Roger Carpenter from Wichita, Kansas. I had beaten Roger once in competition, but he was the kind of guy that would always hurt you even if you won. This time he hurt me and won the match too. So when I left to go back to Denton, Texas, I was sure that I lost the opportunity to go to Korea.

Ahn Ye Mo was the tournament director and the Mission Leader for the US Team going to Korea. He, or someone from his school, contacted me and offered me a spot on the US team. Apparently, Roy Kurban, who earned a spot on the team in that qualifier, had relinquished his spot on the team and the spot was now being offered to me. In May of 1973, all of the team members and coaches were to meet in Los Angeles. I was informed that I had to pay my own air fare to Los Angeles, but the rest of the expenses were to be covered from there. So I met my teammates at the LA airport and the only guys that I actually knew were Roger Carpenter and Howard Jackson. I met Albert Cheeks, Joe Hayes, and Mike Warren, along with several other team competitors. These guys were the standouts and top fighters from the east coast of the United States.

Left at the Airport

Almost all of the competitors were from schools with Korean instructors or coaches that were also going to Korea for this event. This was the very first World Tae Kwon Do Championships and it was a pretty big deal for the Koreans to bring a team from the USA to compete here. There was a U.S. West Coast Team and a U.S. East Coast Team represented. Each team had five team members and an alternate in case of sickness or injury. Finally, it came time to board the 747 aircraft and start the journey to Korea

The Korean's were all shuffling around in the airport giving out the tickets that were purchased to their guys and team members. A big discussion suddenly arose among the Koreans concerning the fact that they did not have enough money to purchase all of the tickets for the teams to go to Korea. I was a little dismayed; because I had to pay my own way to get this far and now they were passing the hat for more contributions to make up the difference needed. I did kick in some more money and thought that the experience would be worth it, but I was tapped out and I could not put any more money in after that. Suddenly, Jack Hwang from Oklahoma City, stepped up and stated that he would pay the $3,000 that they needed for the tickets. For this contribution, Jack would have to be the Mission Leader for his contribution. When Ahn Ye Mo heard the offer he went ballistic. He shook his head, put his face in his hands, turned in circles, and almost broke out in tears. Apparently it was a pretty big deal in Korea to be the Mission Leader and he did not want to relinquish his position. He had no other choice and he relented. Jack Hwang put up the money and became the Mission Leader and pretty soon everyone appeared happy - except Ahn Ye Mo. The coach for the U.S. Teams was Myung Kyu Kang and team manager was Ken Min. The official advisors were Richard Chun and DH Kim.

Now we had tickets being passed out to all of the team travelers. As the group started boarding the plane there were two of us who had not received their boarding passes. Those guys were Howard Jackson and I. Howard had already made a big name for himself in martial arts competitive events. Later that year, he became the first African-American number one Black Belt competitor in the nation rated by Professional Karate magazine. He trained under Joe Lewis and Chuck Norris. He and I struck up a pretty good friendship from the time we were together on this trip and later on when we both competed on a US Team in Europe one year later. As the final Koreans in charge were boarding the plane, they told us to hang tight and they would get us boarding passes for the flight to Korea once they were all inside the plane. Howard and I watched as they closed the door to the 747, we watched as the plane was pushed out onto the runway, we watched as the plane taxied down the runway and we watched as the plane took off for Korea.

Totally disappointed, Howard and I discussed the letdown, but I was more bummed out than he was. Not only did I pay to get there from Dallas, I added more of my money to pay for tickets that I did not get. Howard lived in California so he did not have as far to go as I did. He was still wearing his Marine Corp uniform because he had just gotten his discharge and came straight to the airport. As we discussed our mutual problem, the intercom issued an announcement for me to come to the ticket desk. Howard and I went to the counter and they informed us that the flight had developed hydraulic problems and was returning to the airport. They told me that I had a ticket, because the Koreans on board scrambled and put together enough money to buy my ticket. They did not have a ticket for Howard and he did not get to go. I always wondered what kind of an impact Howard would have made on our team if he could have replaced Archie Cole on our East coast team.

The airlines put me on a baggage carrier cart and took me out on the runway once the plane returned. I scampered up the portable stairs and joined the rest of the group on the plane. Everyone cheered as I boarded the plane, but no one was as pleased as I was to be there. The hydraulic problems were repaired and the plane took off in an hour or so. Already I had beaten amazing odds just to make this trip

Meeting the US Team

On the plane, I was able to visit and get to know other members of my team. I had read many magazine articles on "Jumping" Joe Hayes and his aerial kicking attacks that he used out on the East coast and here I am on the same team with a star competitor. I also met Mike Warren for the first time. Mike was one of the most talented Karate competitors that I have ever met. His speed and body control was amazing and he influenced me greatly with his kicking skills and abilities. Albert Cheeks was about my size and had already accomplished notoriety on the East coast by winning several events. I asked the guys if they had their own Tae Kwon Do studio in New York and they looked at me as if it would be blasphemy for them to have their own school. It was simply not an option. They were so loyal to their instructor that they would not conceive opening their own place - EVER.

My instructor is Grand Master J. Pat Burleson a 10th degree Black Belt in Fort Worth, Texas. I am ever loyal and grateful to Pat for instruction, mentoring, friendship, and the business guidance he has given me over the years. It was always expected that someday you would leave the temple and make your own way in the world through martial arts instruction. I have been blessed to make a living doing something that I know about and enjoy.

Archie Cole was the other team mate on our East Coast "A" Team, he was from Ahn Ye Mo's school in Richardson, Texas. I spent a lot of the travel time with my friend Roger Carpenter from Wichita, Kansas on the flight and during our stop in Japan and obviously in Seoul, Korea. Roger was on the US "B" Team or West coast team, along with Fred Absher and Mike Ajay from New Mexico, Chris Doubek from Colorado, and Bobby Martin from Texas. I did not hang out with those guys much and did not have as close an experience with them.

When we finally arrived in Seoul, I was surprised by the military presence at the airport. The soldiers were all looking to the north hanging on to large mounted weapons as if attack action from the North Koreans was going to happen any minute. Fortunately nothing was going on, they were just ready if it did. After we recovered from the trip, the Korean coaches in charge of our team took us out to train in the streets of Seoul. They would run us down the streets in uniform, occasionally stopping at an intersection to work us out so that the citizens could get a good look at the United States team. We also stopped at some training facilities to work out, but the things that they had us do were not as constructive as they could have been. No discussions about fighting strategy, no combinations that might be effective with these rules, no defensive strategy or mention of team match position. We just did exercises that I believe did not help us in our team goals. We were taken to several Korean restaurants to eat, but I think this benefited the Korean's who had been away from home and did not have this type of food available to them in the states. It was way too spicy and hot for me, I ate sparingly. Toward the end of the trip we were able to eat at a nice hotel and that is where I had my best meal. They served us water at the table and, without thinking, I drank my glass of water. When they say, "Don't drink the water!" They mean it. My return to the United States kept me close to the bathroom for days.

Team Competition in the Kukki-Won

On the first day of the competition we were taken by bus to the Kukki-Won. It was and is the headquarters of Tae Kwon Do. I was told that in Korea there is the judicial system, the military, and Tae Kwon Do. It is the largest export of the country and you will find a Tae Kwon Do school in every major city of the US and throughout the world. At that time, in 1973, the Kukki-Won was a building on a hill with no other buildings around it. When we were transported to the event on the final day there were scores of people standing around for about a mile in every direction. They were all there trying to get a glimpse of the dignitaries and competitors coming to the event. The competition area was huge and the gymnasium where the event was held would only seat around 3,000 people. Only the highest class of spectators could get in. The president of the country and top political personnel and military elite were seated at the show. We had rehearsals and then marched in with our American flag and had to stage in a certain order. It was much like I would imagine the Olympics to be if I had attended such an event.

30

The Central Taekwondo Gymnasium
also known as the "Kukki Won"

Mid U.S. Team?

To our amazement, another U.S. team was introduced at the event and was labeled as the Mid U.S. Team. A Tae Kwon Do man named Sell had financed this team. It included his son, and had he negotiated or paid for admission for his team from Michigan to be allowed to enter the event. I do not know how or why they were admitted, but it happened. We were not friendly with that group as we did not feel that they should be there. They participated in no eliminations as we had, and did not earn the right to attend, in our view. The Mexico team eliminated the Mid U.S. team in the first round of competition.

East U.S. Team against West U.S. Team

On the first day of the World Tae Kwon Do Championship competition, a drawing was held and teams were bracketed to fight each other. My team, the U.S. East Team, drew a bye in the first round, but had to compete against the West US team in the second round. We were pretty depressed about the pairing. We traveled across the world to fight fellow Americans in the second round? Our U.S. East team won, but I do not remember who I fought or what the scoring was at the completion of the matches. The U.S. West team had already fought and won one team match against Singapore before fighting us.

31

Team Competition Bracketing

The bracketing for the First World Tae Kwon Do Championship team matches were as follows:

1st round of competition

Hong Kong vs. Korea = *Korea wins*
Germany wins with a bye

Singapore vs West US = *West US wins*
East US wins with a bye

Khmer vs China = *China wins*

Mid US vs Mexico = *Mexico wins*

France vs. Uganda = *Uganda wins*
Sabah winner with a bye

2nd round of competition

Germany vs. Korea = *Korea wins*

West US vs. East US = *East Us wins*

China vs. Mexico = *Mexico wins*

Uganda vs. Sabah = *Uganda wins*

3rd round of competition

Korea vs. East US = *Korea wins*

China vs. Uganda = *China wins*

4th round of competition

Korea vs. China = *Korea wins*

The winner of the losers bracket would determine the final team fight against Korea for 1st place.

1st round losers bracket

Germany vs. Hong Kong =
   Germany wins

East US wins with a bye due to higher elimination position

Khmer vs China = *China wins*

Mid US vs Mexico = *Mexico wins*

2nd round losers bracket

Germany vs. East Us = *East Us wins*

China vs Mexico = *China wins*

3rd round losers bracket

East Us vs. China = *East Us wins*

Final Team Match

Korea vs. East Us = *Korea wins*

Tae Kwon Do Officials and Rules

Officials shall include one chief umpire, four deputy umpires who are 4th degree or higher. They record both winning and losing points on the scoring paper and two juries who must render judgment of any error made by the umpires, who are 6th degree or higher. Each match was three rounds of two minutes each, with thirty seconds to rest between rounds. One point was awarded for an attack by the fist, one point was awarded for an attack by the foot to the body and two points were awarded for a foot attack to the head. The matches had four side officials and a referee. The judges on each corner sat in a chair and wore red pants with a blue shirt and a red tie to match their pants. The referee was dressed the same and he started and ended the match. The chief umpire indicated the winner after the scores were tallied by the corner umpires. Each corner umpire made notes at the end of the round, but no indication was given as to who may be ahead at the beginning of the next round. Two coaches were at ringside yelling instructions to the fighters. At the conclusion of the rounds the fighters were joined by the referee in the center of the ring and a hand was raised much like in boxing.

Fighting the Korean Team

The Koreans in that era were pretty racist in their view of African-Americans. I was the only white guy on the team and since I was white, I had to be the anchor man because I must be the best. When the Korean press interviewed me about what I did back here in the United States, I informed them that I owned and operated a Tae Kwon Do studio in Denton, Texas. They told me, "No, you are school teacher!" Because I was not a Korean, I was not qualified to teach Tae Kwon Do. So the bias and racism was established before we even fought a match. All of the fighters wore a red or a blue Tae Kwon Do sparring vest to designate each team. No coverings were allowed on our hands or feet and head gear was not allowed. No kicks were allowed to the groin, but we all wore protective cups, supporters and mouthpieces. The matches started and two of my team members, Joe Hayes and Archie Cole lost their matches.

Archie Cole lost his bout to Jung-tae Kim by penalty points for punching in the face. The match with Mike Warren and the Korean guy was an obvious victory for Mike Warren. At the end of the three rounds the referee held up both hands, resulting in a tie. The place erupted in boo's as it was obvious that Mike was the superior fighter in that match. Albert Cheeks match also resulted in a tie. I was nervous about my performance and my focus was on the fact that I would be fighting the anchor man, and he was their best guy.

Establishing the Korean Team

The way that the Korean team was assembled was pretty intense. The organizers of the team divided the country into 12 regions. Each region developed a champion through competitive fighting in their region. Then each of these champions met each other and lived in a together camp for 30 days. They wore the same uniforms every day, they all got up and trained at daybreak, they ate together, they ran up the mountain, they kicked and punched trees, they fought each other and they all slept in tents. At the end of the 30 days they fought in an elimination event to determine their team. These six men, five team members and an alternate assembled into a new camp for 30 more days and trained together in the same manner. When the first World Tae Kwon Do Championships were held these guys were mentally and physically at their peak and would prefer to die rather than lose in this event. *My team met at the airport.*

When I fought the Korean, Jung Do Choi, I hit him with solid body punches when I could. He was relentless with his kicking attack and tried to slam powerful round kicks into my body. Since I am left handed, we faced each other in an open stance (my right foot forward to his left foot forward), and I would slide back from his attack, block his kick and hit him with punches. I often could make a guy lose his air or take a knee in competitions in the US with body punches, but through the body armor I could not slow the Korean down. To get a knock out to the head with a kick was what everyone tried to accomplish. A head punch that disabled your opponent would be a double disqualification. You would be out of the competition and so would he. At the conclusion of the three rounds, my opponent and I assembled in the center of the ring and the referee held up his hand, I had lost. I thought that I had outscored him, but I did not. The Korean team advanced to the final match and our team went to the loser's bracket.

Fighting in the Losers Bracket

The loss in the first round put the U.S. East Coast team into the loser's bracket. This meant that we could fight our way back into the finals and if we kept winning then we would face Korea again in the final match. We fought Germany and won, and I remember getting smacked in the face with a round kick that gave me some swelling on my cheek and eye. We won that team fight and advanced to the third round. The significant match that bears repeating was our fight with the Republic of China. I mentioned earlier that if you knocked out your opponent with a punch to the head it would bring about a double disqualification. You and your fallen opponent would both be disqualified.

In the first match Joe Hayes was leading the match. He punched his guy in the face and the Chinese guy fell to the floor. I think he may have really been hurt because the punch was solid. That resulted in a double disqualification. Archie Cole and his opponent fought to a draw and that kept the matches even with no advantage for either team. Mike Warren punched his guy to the face, probably by accident, and the guy also fell to the floor. These fighters were much smaller on the Republic of China team and I suspect that each of them saw an opportunity to avoid injury and damage by lying down on the floor when they got punched in the head. Well, for whatever reason, either because he was hurt or wanted to lie there, Mike Warrens guy did not get up. When Albert Cheeks opponent had contact with a hand around the head he also went down. Each time the Chinese Team members fell to the floor the medical team came out and put them on a stretcher and carted them off of the floor.

As I approached the ring for my match, the Korean coaches for our team all approached me to remind me that all of my teammates were disqualified along with the Chinese team to this point and the victory or loss was on my shoulders. I understood the situation before they even approached me. The Chinese guy that I fought, Liou. Jyh Horng, was the biggest on their team, but he was not intimidating at all to me.

Horng and I fought for two rounds and I hit him with some pretty good shots. One time, I hit him with a defensive turning back kick, which was one of my most devastating techniques, and dropped him to the floor. The body

35

protectors that we wore kept the strike from being as damaging as I hoped it would be and he returned to his feet pretty quickly. I knew that after two rounds I had to be pretty far ahead. My coaches were pleased and continued to tell me not to punch. When we started the third and final round I did not consider that the Chinese team might have a different plan about punching to the head. Sometime in that final round the Chinese guy jumped up and smacked me as hard as he could with a punch on the chin. He hoped to knock me out, but all he did was make my butt hit the floor and slide across the ring a little. I sat there rubbing my chin. I looked at my Chinese opponent and thought *"Yeah, we can do that!"* My coaches jumped up close to the ring and started yelling *"No, no, you no punch face!"* I understood the strategy of the Chinese, knock the U.S. guy out or we will lose. Make him punch you in the face and we can eliminate the U.S. team with another double disqualification, which probably would seem like a victory to the Chinese team. I got back up to my feet and decided not to throw a single punch for the rest of the fight. When time expired, the center referee called us to the center of the ring and he raised my hand as the victor. The US team then advanced in the loser's bracket to fight Korea for the championship on the final day.

Korea vs. United States Final Team Match

May 27, 1973 was the date of the finals for the first World Tae Kwon Do Championships. It was awesome! The president of the country, Park Chung Hee, the president of the Tae Kwon Do Association, Un Young Kim and all of the Korean military and political dignitaries and officials were there along with their media and TV. After marching in with our flag and all of the ceremony that they had organized for this event, we were ready to get started.

We approached the ring to fight the Korean team again for the final match. We already had experience with these guys from the first matches on the opening day. We fought the same guys and in the same order that we did earlier. The notable difference about our fights concerned Mike Warren. As I stated earlier, I have been around the best and toughest sparring competitors in the nation during my time as a competitor. I never fought Mike in competition, but only as we trained for this event. I never felt like he really applied himself against me in those sessions, but my time with him and observation of his skills make me believe that he was at his very best in personal ability.

36

There was room for only three thousand spectators in the Kukki-Won to observe these championships and the spectators were obviously biased toward the Korean contingent. But at the conclusion of Mike Warrens match against Uee Sung Kang, when the referee raised Mike's hand as the winner the entire place showed their pleasure with loud cheering. Mike had clearly kicked this boys butt in this match and his match was the third of five for the day. The match with Albert Cheeks went down as a defeat for our team and then it was my turn. My match against Jung Do Choi was almost a carbon copy of the first time I had fought against him. Except now he was a little more cautious as the win was going to happen for Korea regardless of the outcome of my match with him. When the three rounds were completed they scored my match with the Korean as a tie.

Our U.S. team won 2nd place out of 26 competing countries and it was quite an accomplishment and experience. We returned to our lives back in the U.S. and I only saw my team members again when I received my award and was inducted into the Tae Kwon Do Hall of Fame on April 6, 2007. I was invited to come back to compete again on the US team in 1975 in Seoul, Korea, as the event was scheduled for every two years, but I declined the offer.

It is my belief that the movie made in the 90's called *"Best of the Best"* was made with the first World Tae Kwon Do event in mind. Much of the story line falls in place with our adventures in Korea.

Another US Team

In late 1973, I sold my Denton Karate studio and I came to Oklahoma City to work for Mike Anderson. Mike had four studios and was deep into his organization and management of Professional Karate Magazine. I took over as general manager and made daily visits each of our studios and taught advanced classes. Joe Lewis came to Oklahoma City to visit Mike and I had the opportunity to work out and spar with Joe while he was in town. Joe was very intimidating to me. I had read about him in the first Black Belt Magazine I purchased when I was a white belt and noted the stories about his awesome side kick and fighting ability. It was said that some competitors would leave the tournament that they had registered for after seeing Joe destroy his first opponent. Especially if they were in the same bracket that he was in.

I sparred with Joe one evening in one of our advanced classes and hit him in the face with a defensive front leg heel kick. I was kind of concerned that he may retaliate and put some hurt on me, but we continued to spar and we all got a great workout. After the session, Joe gave me some respect. He told me that he had just returned from Washington D.C. and had worked out with Jeff Smith, Michal Coles, Pat Worley and all of the great kickers that they had in the Jhoon Rhee organization and that no one had hit him in the head with a kick. Even though Joe was not an outwardly friendly guy to me, I understood that he appreciated my abilities a little bit.

In 1974 sport karate was booming with the ratings in Professional Karate Magazine and everyone was waiting for the next big event. I was selected to be on another US Karate Team that was assembled with probably the greatest stars in karate history. I was fortunate enough to go and be a part of the "Dream Team," with Joe Lewis, Bill Wallace, Jeff Smith, and Howard Jackson. The team and additional demonstrators including Hidy Ochiai, Jim Harrison, Karyn Turner, Al and Malia Dacascos, Jhoon Rhee, Fumio Demura, Takayuki Mikami, and others were assembled by Mike Anderson to fight and demonstrate skills in West Berlin and George Bruckner's big event at the Duetschlandhalle. This was the biggest sports event hall in West Berlin. I kept a diary of daily events and I will tell you some of the highlights now.

The 1974 U.S. Karate Dream Team

Our team met up in Greensboro, North Carolina on May 9, 1974 for a tournament that we all competed in before leaving for Europe. Howard Jackson won the lightweight division, Bill Wallace won the middleweight, Jeff Smith won the light heavyweight, and I won the heavyweight division over Lawrence Huff of Athens, Georgia 3 to 1.

Joe Lewis met us in Germany one day after we arrived. We went over to George Bruckner's sport center to teach a clinic on karate technique and one German guy challenged Howard Jackson because he did not believe that his combination would work. Howard sparred with him and kicked him in the head and the guy became very humble after that. I had a great time running the streets with my teammates until early in the morning almost every night. We worked out together, but not too intensely, after all, the ego's in this group

38

The U.S. Dream Team: *Bill Wallace, Howard Jaxkson, Jeff Smisth, Jim Butin and Joe Lewis*

could fill a blimp. Joe Lewis did teach me a lot about broken rhythm training. Howard Jackson's ability to employ this strategy is well known. This was the longest time that I had spent around Joe, and I always admired his tenacity and skills.

Joe's people skills in my opinion at that time were not great, he was not a very friendly guy and I felt uncomfortable in his presence and did not enjoy his personality. Howard Jackson was a genuine good guy, I loved his attitude and willingness to share anything he had with you that would help you. Jeff Smith was so well rounded, he could punch effectively with either hand, his cardio was always great and his kicking power was awesome. Jeff took pride in being able to wear out almost anybody in the ring. I had a lot of experience with Jeff in the ring before this trip and we held a mutual respect for each other. Bill Wallace was special, he beat me for 1st place in the two championship matches in which we fought in the U.S. Karate Championships in Dallas, Texas in 1971 and 1973. Each time we fought I planned on beating Bill and each time I got 2nd place in overtime. I kicked Bill in the face, and took his air with a body punch, but I did not beat him.

When the U.S. team showed up to compete in the big show, we were blown away by the large banner advertising the event. It was hung on the side of the building that the event was held in and the banner was four stories tall. It was a picture of Joe Lewis performing his famous jump side kick with his hair flying and on a black background with German advertising about the event.

The banner advertising the U.S. Team event was almost four stories tall!

Joe had to be impressed with this testament to his notoriety. The event was packed and I have no clue as to how many the center held. When the American team assembled for the show, we had no idea who the German team had on their squad. We all lined up with our Stars and Stripes uniforms which were specially made for our team by Mike Anderson.

Our US team fought the German team that evening around 9:00 p.m. I again fought the anchor position, but that spot was supposed to be reserved for Joe Lewis. Joe approached me as the matches began and after we had a chance to see our competition, he was slated to fight a guy who was about 6'3" or 6'4" and around 225 pounds. My original guy was about 6' tall or so and I thought I would do well against him. Joe wanted me to switch fights with his guy but I didn't want to. His guy was big and Joe said to me that he had trouble with big guys. I thought that the pressure of being on the giant poster out front and all of the advertising about Joe Lewis being the star of the event maybe got to him a little. I did not want to fight his guy, but I relented and made the switch. There was a lot of pressure on me with these teammates of mine.

Howard Jackson won his match 4 to 0, then Bill Wallace won his match 5 to 0, then Jeff Smith won his match 5 to 0, and Joe Lewis beat what was supposed to be my guy 5 to 0. None of our guys even got scored on, and in fact the guys were making fun of Howard for only getting 4 points. So I knew that I was going to be the object of abuse and have fun made of me for the rest of the trip if I did not perform as well as they did. Like a man possessed, I was all over my guy Ivan Oliviari and beat him 5 to 0, just like most of my teammates. So we beat the German team 24-0 and Howard was the slacker. We all abused him for days for only scoring 4 points.

The next team fight we had was also in Berlin at an air force base where we fought a Dutch team and won by a score of 22 to 1. We finished the show, which included me hitting Hidy Ochiai with a sledge hammer as he lay on a bed of nails with slabs of concrete on his stomach. We soon left there to travel to Amsterdam and drove all night to get there. We toured the red light district of Amsterdam, the sex shops were loaded with stuff you wouldn't believe. There in the red light district, the call girls are all housed in cubicles with

This crescent kick missed... but Ivan Oliviari lost the match 5-0

picture windows and curtains. They would show off their goods, then close the shades if you made a deal. We went to a live sex show in Amsterdam. The seats were stadium style like a movie theater. After a while some of the girls would come off of the stage and go into the audience. If they picked you, you could go up on the stage and have sex with them in front of everyone for free. One girl came over to me and grabbed me by the arm to go with her on stage. You have never seen a guy fight so hard to stay in his chair. We did a lot of shopping for stuff and I brought back some pretty cool things. I bought a cuckoo clock that was really intricate and ornate and paid to have it shipped it back to the United States. All the guys made fun of me because they were all sure that I would never see that clock or my $80 again. It arrived at my house a couple of weeks after I did. We took a neat group picture in Holland dress and had a great time sightseeing and visiting the area.

We fought another Dutch team in Rotterdam and beat them 45 to 8. I won my match 6 to 0 and knocked my guy out. Several members of our troop left to return to the US including Bill Wallace. We then returned to Amsterdam.

Members of our US fighting and demo team: Top – Jeff Smith, Me, Jim Harrison, Karyn Turner, Mr. Crane, Malia Dacascos

Bottom: Our tour guide, Al Dacascos. Linda Lee, Howard Jackson, Bobby Crane

Hotel Kras Napolsky

We fought another Dutch team in Amsterdam at the Hotel Kras Napolsky and beat them 23 to 1 without Bill Wallace. I won my match 3 to 0. Before the team matches, Jeff Smith and I were standing around upset because all of the team members that we were fighting were colored belts. There was a black guy standing close to us, his name was Peter Kredit, and Jeff asked him "Where are the Black Belts?" The guy responded that there were black belts there. Jeff asked if he was a Black Belt and he said "yes." Jeff then asked him, "Why don't you fight then?" The guy responded that there were no black belts worth fighting against. Jeff got a big grin on his face and then walked over to the announcer and told him about the conversation and challenged this guy on the microphone. Then this black guy unbuttoned his shirt and pulled off one shoe and postured like *"Don't make me come over there, or you will be sorry!"* The crowd and the man on the microphone were really egging this whole situation on. So the fight was on. The guy remained in his street clothes, but took off his shirt. He and Jeff were both bare knuckle and started fighting on the stage. For the first thirty or forty seconds the guy held his own against Jeff, and then Jeff started landing big blows. The guy went down, and he was unconscious. Then two guys grabbed him by his ankles and pulled him off the stage. The crowd loved it, but I was concerned that maybe we should be cautious. After all, we did not speak the language and we were in a foreign country. There were a couple of other fights that broke out in the audience, but we were not involved. Our team fought in two more team events both in Rotterdam and won easily. In the last event, which we won 45 to 4, I won my match over supposedly Holland's best karate man 3 to 1. On May 28th I caught my flight home.

Professional Ranking

I knew that I would achieve a higher rating after beating both John Natividad and Jeff Smith for the Light Heavyweight National Championship and becoming the Grand Champion in the Top Ten Nationals in 1974.

I had hoped that I would finally make that "Top Five" list, which was where I believed the power was. In the next ratings in the Professional Karate Magazine, the ranking list changed. Each weight category featured a top ten by weight class. I was rated #2 in the light heavyweight division and was happy to be there, but I always wondered where I might have been ranked if the top 20 had continued for at least one more posting.

My greatest day as a pro, this match against
John Natividad and the final against Jeff Smith

Louis Arnold and I in the
US Championships in Dallas

Louis Arnold

One of my top brown belts and best friend George Bray, went with me to most of the tournaments in the early 70's. If I won 1st in Black Belt, it was pretty common for George to win 1st place in Brown Belt. One of George's toughest foes was a man named Louis Arnold from Austin, Texas. I watched George fight him and it always seemed that George got the best of him. One year in the late 70's after Louis Arnold advanced to black belt, I was competing in the US Championships in Dallas and drew Louis in a preliminary match. I figured that I had his number after all of the times that I had watched George fight him, but I was in for a surprise.

The photo of me hitting him with a solid front thrust kick is about the only definitive strike that I put on Louis that day. I won the match, but after seeing the video of the fight, he was constantly coming after me as I strategically withdrew to avoid his attacks. I am glad that I did not have to fight with him in any future matches.

Break-ins

In the late 70's, my small karate studio had a rash of break-ins. The thieves took mostly cheap merchandise like throwing stars, nunchakus, and some cash was stolen. The thief would come in sometime during the night through a bathroom window, after he busted it out. I tried to secure the window by installing Angle Iron and anchor bolts in the wall to keep from experiencing repeat performances, but it did not seem to matter. So after the sixth break in occurred, I decided to solve the problem. I told myself that I would be just as committed to catching this guy as he was to breaking in. During these break ins, my silver medal from the first World Tae Kwon Do Championships that I had on display in the entry area from Korea, and the samurai sword that was presented to me as an award for the victorious team competition that I participated on in Europe were also stolen. Each night for about a week, I left the karate studio after classes, went home to eat, watched a movie, played some video games and then at around 12:00 a.m. I returned and quietly snuck back into the studio. I went into a back room with no windows and worked on my business books or read until 6:00 a.m. Then I left to go home and sleep for a while.

One Thursday at 3:00 am, while I was working on my books for the month, I heard the window in the bathroom break out. The karate studio was situated so that I could look into the bathroom from the entry way and see into the bathroom from the reflection in the mirror. I had left the door open and the light on so that I could clearly see anyone coming in. I had my two friends with me, Smith & Wesson and their cousin Dan Wesson, and plenty of ammo. I was sure that I was about to shoot somebody. The thief waited about 20 minutes before coming in to make sure that the broken glass did not alert anyone. When he finally slithered in through the broken window, I could see a screw driver in his hand and a buck knife on his belt but I did not see any other weapons.

At that time I owned a coke machine that I operated on the honor system. You lifted the lid, took a coke, and put your money in the tray inside the box. This guy lifted out the money tray and was dumping it in his hands when I came around the corner about 10 feet away with the hammer back on my .357 Dan Wesson. I said, "If you pass gas, you die!" Clint Eastwood should have used that line. I was fully prepared to shoot this guy, but he did the right thing. If he would have run back toward the window, I would have shot him. If he would have come toward me, I would have shot him. Instead, he fell to the floor, dropped the money and started crying. I made him lay on his stomach with his hands behind his back and hand cuffed him. At this point, I knew I was not going to shoot him, but I did mess with him for a while. I told him that I had to shoot him because he was in my place and had taken my things. I then put the gun on his knee and told him that after I shoot him in the knee he would limp as he walked for the rest of his life. Then I put it on his right shoulder and told him he would not write very well or be able to skip rocks across the water after I blew his shoulder apart. He said he had to pee, and I told him that it was just as easy for me to clean up blood as it was to clean up piss, so he better hold his water. I stood him up and told him that I was going to show him how they made Chuck Norris movies. I hit him in the head with a round kick and knocked him down, but I promise you that I have hit guys that I like harder than I hit this guy. After about 30 minutes or so, I called the police and they arrived and seemed amazed that this guy was not shot or dead. After every break in, I filed a police report, so I am sure that they were looking for a corpse when they arrived. I never got any of my stolen items back, but I was never broken into again either.

Sum Young Guy

I am sure that almost all of the karate studio owners that are reading this have some similar story about guys who come into their studios and want to test you. I have had a few and one story that I remember involved a guy who said he wanted to take classes, but did not want to join if he could whip me. I thought about the liability of just thumping him, so I had him use sparring equipment on his hands and feet, but no head gear or mouthpiece. I figured that this was a free private lesson if anyone had to ask. I moved around with him for a while and after his back hit the mirror, I was glad that the mirror did not break. I don't recall how many times I hit him before he asked me to stop, but it couldn't have been longer than a minute or so. He then said he was ready to sign up and become a member in our karate program. I told him that we did not have any openings for new members at that time and that he should leave. I never saw him again.

Dave Ruppert

During the 80's a lot of guys came and went. One story I remember well involved a man named David Ruppert. Dave was a top competitor in the upper Midwest and was involved with Mike Dillard here in Oklahoma. I would see him when I picked up merchandise over at Century Martial Arts Supply, and he asked me about coming over to spar with me sometime. I was agreeable to a visit from Dave whenever he could come by and one day he showed up. Dave was around 6'5" and had some amazing reach with both punching skills and kicking ability. As I sized him up, I tried to determine the best way to establish an advantage with him. I decided that when he tried to hit me with a round kick to the head, I would hit him with a defensive side kick to the groin. The idea was to intimidate him and make him keep his long legs on the ground and take away his kicking reach advantage. With tall guys that idea is one of the few strategies that will work if they are predominantly kickers. Well, my plan achieved success and I speared Dave in the groin when he attempted the head kick. He immediately fell to the ground clutching his groin area. I quickly said, "Dave, don't tell me that you are not wearing a cup!" He nodded and groaned that he was not wearing one. I thought to myself, where else could you hit a guy that is 6'5" other than the groin and I was surprised that he was not prepared for that eventuality. He sat there on the floor in my studio for 30 minutes or so and could not get any better. He limped out of the studio to his car and drove away.

I never sparred with Dave again, but there is more to the story. He was staying at Mike Dillard's house and was still feeling a lot of pain when he got there. Dave dragged himself from his car to the front door and rang the doorbell because he couldn't stand up to open the door on his own. Mike Dillard heard the doorbell and looked out the peep hole on his door and saw no one, so he went back to his living room and sat down. When the doorbell rang again, Mike thought it was kids pulling a prank. This time he opened the door and found Dave Ruppert sitting down on the ground, Mike then helped him in and heard the story.

Flennoy Milling

Flennoy was not a great competitor in my view. A man earns that distinction with longevity in the sport by winning and displaying his skills over a period of years. Flennoy could fight pretty well and could use a variety of kicks when he fought in competition and he placed in Oklahoma events pretty consistently. One winter, when I had the flu, Flennoy came in to my studio and wanted to spar with me. At that time I had never refused an offer to fight with anybody, even if I wasn't feeling well. So, even though I did not feel well, I put on my gear and I sparred with him for a while. I am sure that he got the best of me because of my sickness that day. After we finished sparring he left and I went home to bed. About a week or so later, Flennoy called and wanted to come over to spar again, I agreed and he brought an entourage of 10 or more people to watch him kick my ass. By this time I had recovered from the flu and was ready to party. That day I hit Flennoy with every technique in my book. I would say that I embarrassed him in front of his home boys. In fact I hit him with so many techniques that he asked to stop sparring. He never came back to spar with me again.

There is an additional interesting note about Flennoy. He was riding in a car with his buddies one night when a .22 caliber gun discharged from the back seat of the car in which he was riding and shot Flennoy in the back of the head. You would think that his friends would take him to the hospital since they were all buddies, but instead they just opened up the car door and pushed Flennoy out on to the pavement at the local 7-Eleven convenience store. He survived the gunshot wound to the head but the doctors didn't take the bullet out because they were afraid of more damage to his brain. He continued to compete in local tournaments and finally at my urging, the area promoters decided it was not worth the liability to have him compete in their events and he was banned from many of the karate tournaments in Oklahoma.

Dale Cook

Dale Cook competed in most of my early tournaments that I hosted in Oklahoma City back in the 70's, and as he got older he was quite a factor in the PKA and WKA full contact events all over the world. I was feeling pretty good about my boxing skills in the late 70's and invited Dale to come in and move around with me some time. He did show up one evening and I thought that I was going to have some fun with him. We boxed only - no kicking. I thought that I had better take it easy on Dale since he was smaller than me and typically fought welterweight or middleweight events and I was a light heavy weight. After 15 minutes or so, I realized that I could not hit Dale with any of my combinations and he could pepper me with shots just about any time he wanted to. My respect for Dale expanded after that experience and Dale went on to become the greatest full contact karate champion ever to come out of Oklahoma. He briefly pursued a boxing career as well. He still promotes MMA and kickboxing events in Oklahoma and operates karate studios in the Tulsa area.

Max Alsop

In the 80's, I remember fighting a guy that I had watched competing in the heavyweight division. I would never choose to fight with this guy by choice. Max Alsop was from Dallas and outside of the ring he was the friendliest, nicest guy that you could talk to. In the ring this 6'3" guy weighing 230 pounds with a 34" waist and built massively strong, would look at you with beady black eyes with the intent of taking you apart. I remember that Max hit me during my match with him using a punch to the chin that made me slide backwards on the seat of my pants like a cartoon character for about ten feet.
As I lay there on my back rubbing my chin, I realized that he had sprung my jaw hinge on each side. I could not chew meat for two weeks after that match. When my senses returned I thought that at the very least the judges

would give me a point for face contact or excessive contact. Instead, when I returned to my feet they gave a point to him! I thought, Oh, no – they're going to reward him for that? I then feared that I was going to get more of the same. I don't have a clue what happened for the rest of the match, but out of total desperation and fear for my life, I must have mounted some decent attacks because I won the match.

Tony Thompson

I fought and won my third national title in the light heavyweight division in the Battle of Atlanta in 1976 and later in 1979 competed in the Diamond Nationals in Minnesota. This tournament was huge and had a lot of black belt talent competing that I had not seen before. My match before the finals was against a California fighter named Tony Thompson. Tony was a big black guy that looked formidable and I was cautious with him. I tried scoring when I could but I did not dominate him during the match. I engaged with him and scored a quick back fist strike, when he rang my bell with a punch that gave me a "flash." When you talk to boxers they will tell you that the "flash" usually indicates that you are about to be knocked out if you catch too many more serious blows. The time expired on the match and my back fist gave me the victory by one point. My thoughts after walking away from the ring were that Tony didn't feel that he had lost the match and that I was not worthy of his respect.

In the summer of 1980 I fought in Roy Kurban's Pro-Am Karate Championships in Ft. Worth. I did well in the eliminations and was scheduled to fight in the heavyweight final matches that evening. My first match was with Tony Thompson. I remembered the "flash" that Tony had given me before and I was confident that he could do it a second time if I was not prepared. When we bowed in I decided that whenever Tony moved toward me, I would make the commitment to hit him as hard as I could with a ridge hand strike on the side of the head. I was not going to throw any kicks, no body punches, only the ridge hand. I landed that blow several times during the match. Well, that mindset and commitment helped me to win the match and the respect of Tony Thompson. He told me after that fight that, "No white boy had ever hit him that hard!"

I fought in the final match against a big man from Kansas named Dan Martin. The only unusual thing about this match was that with five judges watching, I hit my opponent with a defensive spinning back fist and knocked him unconscious and not one of the judges saw the contact. I probably should have been disqualified, but hey, it was the finals! Once he recovered we continued the match and I won my fourth and final national championship.

I Am A S**t Magnet

During the years that followed, I tried to shift my balance in martial arts away from competition and more toward business. Even though I had great opportunities and accomplishments in competition, I felt that I was a white belt in business. There weren't the opportunities to research and compare karate school business methods, network, or join karate business associations as there are today.

My classes were great and our service in the class room was second to none, but my business structure sucked. I gained some success from my instructor, Pat Burleson and tried to mimic things that he was doing in the Ft. Worth area, but our financial success was limited. My implementation of an EFT (electronic funds transfer) system in 1988 in my studio was probably one of the first in the southwest to develop an automatic payment system.

I seemed to have a black cloud following me during this business era. Because of the people around me in business, I soon developed the attitude that I was a Sh** Magnet! The names of the individuals on this list are fictitious but they know who they are.

ST MAGNET EXAMPLE #1** - I added a business partner, I will call him John in Oklahoma City in 1974. John understood the discount financing business and at that time we sold membership contracts to a local finance company in OKC at a discount. He had been entrenched in the karate business under Mike Anderson before I bought the corporation. John ran one of the three locations that we had at the time, but simply lost interest. He quit working and because of business costs and problems I felt forced to close all but one location as he moved away to sell vacuum cleaners. He has no PERSEVERENCE!

S**T MAGNET EXAMPLE #2 - Next emerged a man named, I will call him Jim, who apparently achieved his black belt in Chicago. Jim was a smooth talker and sold a lot of memberships for me. He encouraged me to open up a south side location so that he could sell twice as many memberships. I committed to a $5,000 TV advertising campaign, opened up the location, and he lost interest, quit working and decided to be a policeman in an outlying town. He has no COMMITMENT!

S**T MAGNET EXAMPLE #3 - I trained and developed a great world champion in the PKA. I will call him Tommy. Tommy came to me as a green belt and made his Black Belt under me, he was a great fighter, but when I placed him in the new location that the previous guy named Jim urged me to open. Tommy had no empathy to the fact that I could not continue to operate the location. I offered to give it to him free and clear, but he refused. I took a loss of about $25,000 on this deal and almost had to file bankruptcy. He went to work for a competitor of mine two miles from my location. He then told anyone who asked him where he received his training from and that he got his Black Belt in the Army. He has no LOYALTY!

S**T MAGNET EXAMPLE #4 - In 1988 one of my students had a father, I will call Vernon and he entered the picture. He convinced me to open another location on the north side of Oklahoma City. He fronted all of the money to open the location and took 49% of the operation for his contribution. I thought I had all of my bases covered, when the police contacted me because Vernon had broken into and stolen martial arts supplies and equipment from an importer that we were purchasing from. He was caught trying to fence off the items and the police and everyone else thought that I was involved because he was my partner. He has no HONESTY!

S**T MAGNET EXAMPLE #5 - In the late 80's one of my Black Belts returned to OKC from Nebraska and taught classes for me in our northwest Oklahoma City location. I will call him Steve. He had a speckled past with the law, but we seemed to get along and he convinced me that he was there for the good of martial arts. In fact, before his black belt exam, I met with the other black belt members of our studio to get their feeling about whether or not we should allow Steve to test for black belt. They all voted that we should

53

kill him. I saw value in Steve and vetoed the option for murder. I was wrong and they were right.

Steve was too militant in his regard for children in the classes he taught and was so strict that we were in danger of losing students. He also made scenes at the area tournaments and showed bad attitude and created negative scenes if the points called did not go his way. Finally, one day I was sparring with him and he came in with a strong attack so I punched him and knocked him down. I apologized for the contact and he said, "That's what I was trying to do to you!" Then he said he was taking his "bad attitude" and getting out of our location.

He later opened up a location five miles from us and bilked a businessman out of $40,000 in about a year. The businessman called to tell me the story. I told him that he should have asked me before he spent so much on Steve to help him get established. He said Steve painted me as a bad guy and that I destroyed his potential to succeed. The man told me that he visited Steve about the fact that he could not put any more money into the location and that it was going to have to make it on its own revenue. Steve said, "If I don't get my paycheck on Friday, I am leaving!" He has no HONOR!

S**T MAGNET EXAMPLE #6 - In the late '70's two parents brought me their 5-year old son, who I will call Richard, to start classes. Richard grew up in our studio and was the son I never had. Richard won over 500 trophies in competition and was well on his way to being the professional Black Belt entrepreneur to succeed me. In 1996 Richard took a young girl out to in a secluded area and gave her alcohol. He was convicted of sexual crimes with a minor. I was so lucky that the news reporters did not get wind of this story at the time or they could have run me out of business. Richard had to go away. He has no DISCIPLINE!

S**T MAGNET EXAMPLE #7 - Another student that made Black Belt with me, I will call him Devin. He was an instructor in my studio. I gave Devin the opportunity to run the advanced and intermediate classes. We discussed the possibility of him operating his own studio in the future. Devin was accused of sexual misconduct with a young girl. He vehemently denied doing anything more than giving her rides home. Even her parents believed him, until later.

He was a legal gun dealer and came in at the conclusion of one of our in house tournaments with the goal of causing a scene. I believe it was to shoot me if I tried to throw him out physically. He had opened up a studio two miles from our current location and enticed many of our membership to come to his school. Remember Allen Steen and Roy Kurban? Devin had learned from me how to conduct the floor and teach the classes, but I never showed him the business operation and his location folded up and closed in a year. He has no LOYALTY!

S**T MAGNET EXAMPLE #8 - The last on my list is a guy I will call Matt. Matt tested for and passed our black belt exam in 1998 or so. One of our post requirements at National Karate Inc. is that we do not issue a diploma for Black Belt until 16 months of probation had passed. This requires the applicant to continue to attend classes, participate in studio activities, and testing duties before receiving certification as a full blown Black Belt. Matt showed up after about a year requesting his diploma. I explained that he had not fulfilled the requirement to participate and that he would receive it after his probation had passed if he was ready to fulfill it starting now. Matt chose to leave and get his Black Belt certificate on the internet from some Yahoo Black Belt selling certificates on line. He has no INTEGRITY!

Long ago I established a list of Black Belts that are no longer associated with me or our organization. We list these men as being "Dismissed with Prejudice!"

Allen Estes

The final year of karate tournaments for me was 1992. I decided I needed a goal for the year and thought that I would strive to be the #1 executive Black Belt in the Oklahoma Karate Association for that year. The goal was not unapproachable, I just needed to compete in six tournaments during the year and do well. I had won three tournaments, when I was getting ready to fight in the fourth event for 1st place against a man named Allen Estes. It seemed that Allen and I were always fighting for the first place spot. I noticed that he was looking at me and getting psyched up for the battle. He had fire in his eyes and he was strategizing as to what he needed to do to wipe me out. He was intensely preparing for battle. Instead of focusing on him, I was thinking about going fishing. At that moment I knew that I should not be there. He wanted it, I just expected to win. I was there to collect a trophy - he was there to kick some butt! I won that final match, but knew that it was my last one.

Regrets

The only regret that I have in my martial arts experience concerns my lack of boxing training early on. I did not train or develop boxing skills until I was in my thirties. I obviously needed some boxing skills in my match with Jeff Smith in 1975 for the Light Heavy weight PKA World title. Jeff TKO'd me in the fifth round, but it was not even a close match. There were no sparring partners, here in Oklahoma City, who could push me or impact the amount of contact on me that Jeff could.

I learned too late that there is something special about putting your head against a guy's chest with your hands up, knowing that he cannot hurt you because of the blocking skills you have achieved. I miss those days of sparring with my good friend and black belt student Troy Cheatwood. We would get together every week in the 90's and fight three to eight rounds, usually twice a week. I often would engage a class of my students and ask them to hit me as hard as they could for two minutes without me hitting them back. I never took a knee or lost my wind.

At 52 years old, I sparred one evening with one of my big brown belts (250 pounds big), normally I could always handle just about anything Ken Wulff could dish out. This time I realized that I could not hit him with any of my combinations and he seemed to smack me just about any time he threw a punch. Regrettably, I decided that if I continued boxing, somebody would eventually hurt me so I hung up the gloves and discontinued my boxing after that.

Now...

I enjoyed my 30 plus years of karate tournament competition and I would not trade anything for the experiences that I have had. I have never looked back or thought that I should have competed more. When I walked away, il felt like I had so much valuable information to share with followers of this amazing sport. I opened up a Karate School in Oklahoma City, operating it for 47 years. It evolved into a hghly successful and profitable school.

Upon my retirement two of my top instructors took over the school, and it is still the best school in the region - **nationalkarateokc.com.**

Please visit my website.. **beyondthefighting.com** I share all of the ideas and techniques for either an existing school or anyone thinking about starting a new school in my book **"Beyond the Fighting"**... *proven succss guidelines for operating a successful Martial Art School.*

JIM BUTIN
BEYOND THE FIGHTING

Jim Butin is available for consulting and lectures in person or online.

Jim Butin, Grand Master 10th Degree Black Belt
beyondthefighting@gmail.com
1-405-202-8701

Visit the website...
beyondthefighting.com

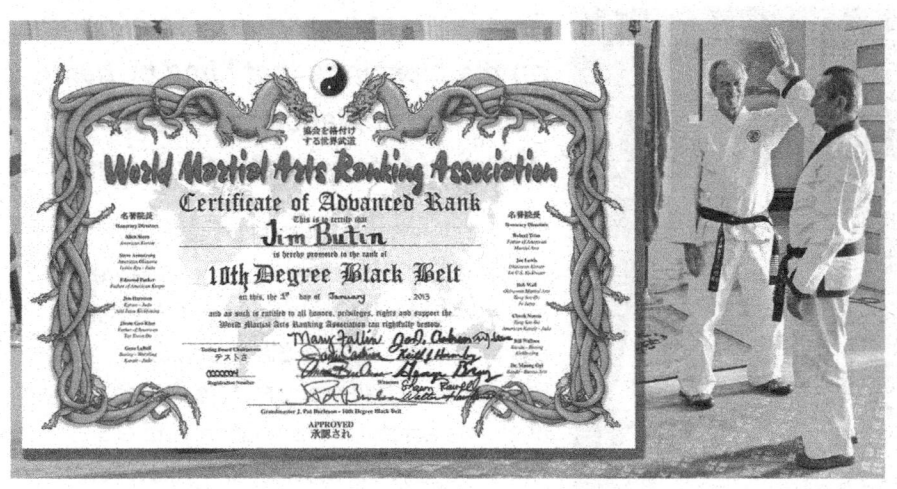

Acceptng my 10th Degree Black Belt ranking
and WMARA diploma from
J. Pat Burleson at the State Capitol of Oklahoma in 2013

The World Martial Arts Ranking Association
was founded and established by
Grand Master 10th Degree J. Pat Burleson
to give credibility and recognition for all legitimate Black Belts
seeking an organization that will recognize leaders in our field
with distinction and the proper notoriety.

Grand Master 10th Degree Black Belt
Jim Butin
beyondthefighting.com

This is great opportunity to expand on the blessings that I had by being under the guidance and instruction of Grand Master J. Pat Burleson.

Sadly J. Pat Burleson passed away on October 31, 2021. Over 1,000 people were in attendance for his viewing and "Celebration of life". A 10th degree Black Belt, Mr. Burleson has had many feature stories about his achievements in local and U.S. News magazines, movies, and Television. He was a movie and stunt actor with regular appearances on the CBS Television show "Walker, Texas Ranger." He traveled the world as a speaker and trainer. He was recently the special training and motivational coach for the Sacramento State football team.

He established the first karate school in 1959 in Ft. Worth, Texas. His dojo not only blazed a trail in the Dallas/Ft. Worth area, but was one of the original karate schools founded in America. His business practices of developing belt programs for karate business was also a first.

History records J. Pat Burleson as America's karate pioneer and "Father" of all karate champions. He won the first U.S. Karate Championships in 1964 in Washington D.C. His karate career began in 1957 in Japan while in the Navy. He holds the highest American Taekwondo ranking under the "father" of American Taekwondo, Jhoon Rhee.

Master Burleson has been estimated to have 250,000 graduates from his karate schools. His influence and guidance over 60 years have been instrumental in the maturity of so many people. Before it was commonly known that martial arts is a tremendous tool for developing solid character and building confidence, respect, and discipline in people, Pat was laying the roadmap for future generations with martial arts principles.

In addition to being an icon to multitudes of karate practitioners, Master Burleson was so admired by the masters of other styles of martial arts

MEMBER

that they have endorsed him as the head of the World Martial Arts Ranking Association and allow their names to be placed on every certificate endorsing the black belt rank of anyone fortunate enough to be awarded a diploma. Many of these men are no longer living which makes this endorsement impossible to achieve through any other ranking organization. They include martial arts icon's such as Allen Steen from American karate, Ed Parker father of American Kenpo, Jim Harrison from Aiki Jutsu kickboxing, Jhoon Goo Rhee father of American Tae Kwon Do, Robert Trias father of American Martial Arts, Joe Lewis Okinawan Karate and the first US Kickboxing Champion, Steve Armstrong from American Okinawan Isshin Ryu, Chuck Norris from Tang Soo Do and American Karate, Bill Wallace from Karate, Judo and American Kickboxing, Bob Wall from Okinawan Karate and Tang Soo Do, and Dr. Maung Gyi from Bando and Burma Arts.

Master Burleson's legacy will exist through the continuation of this association through the guidance of Jim Butin, the support of Anna Burleson and many other leaders in the martial art field. Inquiries for involvement may be forwarded to 5724 Arrowhead NE, Piedmont, Oklahoma 73078 or beyondthefighting@gmail.com

I am proud to say that Master Burleson requested that I take over the position as the head of that prestigious organization. the WMARA

As the Director of the World Martial Arts Ranking Association. (WMARA) I am honored to offer the most credible program for testing for higher rank Black Belts.

*"May God bless you as
he has me my entire life."*

Jim Butin